True Stories Pack 1
Teaching Notes
Thelma Page

Co...

Welcom... ries 2
How to ... 2
Teachin... art) 3
Vocabul... 5

Alex Brychta
The Story of an Illustrator
Group and independent activities 6
Speaking and listening 7
Writing 8

At the Top of the World
The Story of Tenzing Norgay
Group and independent activities 9
Speaking and listening 10
Writing 11

Travels with Magellan
The Story of Ferdinand Magellan
Group and independent activities 12
Speaking and listening 13
Writing 14

Ocean Adventure
The Story of Joshua Slocum
Group and independent activities 15
Speaking and listening 16
Writing 17

The Underground Railroad
The Story of Harriet Tubman
Group and independent activities 18
Speaking and listening 19
Writing 20

High Flier
The Story of Amy Johnson
Group and independent activities 21
Speaking and listening 22
Writing 23

Links to other Oxford Reading Tree titles 24

Welcome to Oxford Reading Tree True Stories!

This new set of books at Stages 8 and 9 has been specially written to provide new biographies of fascinating lives. Children who prefer factual books to fiction will particularly welcome them. The books also provide exciting narratives for those children who love fiction and need to be tempted to broaden their horizons.

In group and individual reading of these stories, the children should be encouraged to develop their understanding and use of non-fiction texts by

- Clarifying their understanding of the difference between fact and fiction
- Learning to skim-read to find particular information
- Practising note-taking to use in their own writing
- Developing their ability to use their own words to give an oral or written report
- Developing their vocabulary and spelling strategies

The books feature a range of men and women from various cultural backgrounds and from different times in history. In pack 1 the range is from Ferdinand Magellan whose story begins in 1519 to Alex Brychta whose adventure begins in 1968. All the stories show that real life can be every bit as exciting as a fictional adventure.

How to introduce the books

- Before reading the story, always read the title and talk about the picture on the cover. Find out what the children already know about the person featured. Read the blurb on the back cover.
- Go through the book together, looking at the pictures and talking about them.
- Read through the words in the glossary together. This lists technical and specialist words related to the person's life and achievements.

Teaching objectives

Curriculum coverage chart

	Speaking and listening	Reading	Writing
Alex Brychta *The Story of an Illustrator*			
Scotland	Levels B/C	Levels B/C	Levels B/C
N. Ireland	Activities a,b,c,f,g,h,i Outcomes: a,b,c,e,f	Activities: a,b,c,e,f,h Outcomes: b,c,d,e,f,g,h,i,k	Outcomes: b,c,h,i
Wales	Range 1,2,3,5 Skills 1,2,3,4,5,6 Language Development: 3	Range 1,2,3,4,5,6 Skills 1,2 Language Development: 1	Range: 1,2,3,4,5,6,7 Skills: 1,2,3,4,5,6,7,8 Language Development: 1,2,3,4
NC/NLS Y2T3	1b, 2e, 3b, 4b	W2 S1 T13	T19
At the Top of the World *The Story of Tenzing Norgay*			
Scotland	Levels B/C	Levels B/C	Levels B/C
N. Ireland	Activities: a,b,c,f,g,h,i Outcomes: a,b,c,e,f	Activities: a,b,c,e,f,h Outcomes: b,c,d,e,f,g,h,i,k	Outcomes: b,c,d,h,i
Wales	Range 1,2,3,5 Skills 1,2,3,4,5,6 Language Development: 3	Range 1,2,3,4,6 Skills 1,2 Language Development: 1	Range 1,2,3,4,5,6,7 Skills 1,2,3,4,5,6,7,8 Language Development: 1,2,3,4
NLS/NC	1e 2b 3a 4a	W1 W3 S3	T1 T2 T11
Travels with Magellan *The Story of Ferdinand Magellan*			
Scotland	Level B/C	Level B/C	Level B/C
N. Ireland	Activities: a,b,c,f,g,h,i Outcomes: a,c	Activities: a,b,c,e,f,h Outcomes: b,c,d,e,f,g,h,i,k	Outcomes: a,b,c,h,i
Wales	Range: 1,2,3,5 Skills: 1,2,3,4,5,6 Language Development: 3	Range: 1,2,4,5,6 Skills:1,2 Language Development: 1	Range:1,2,3,4,5,6,7 Skills:1,2,3,4,5,6,7,8 Language Development: 1,2,3,4
NLS/NC	1c, 2c, 3e, 4b	T1 T15 W7	T20
Ocean Adventure *The Story of Joshua Slocum*			
Scotland	Level B/C	Level B/C	Level B/C
N. Ireland	Activities: a,b,c,f,g,h,i Outcomes: a,b,c,e,f	Activities: a,b,c,e,f,h Outcomes: b,c,d,e,f,g,h,i,k	Outcomes: b,c,h,i
Wales	Range: 1,2,3,5 Skills: 1,2,3,4,5,6	Range: 1,2,3,4,6 Skills: 1,2 Language Development: 1	Range: 1,2,3,4,5,6,7 Skills: 1,2,3,4,5,6,7,8 Language Development: 1,2,3,4
NLS/NC	1e 2b 3e 4a	S1 W8 T7	W10

The Underground Railroad *The Story of Harriet Tubman*			
Scotland	Level B/C	Level B/C	Level B/C
N. Ireland	Activities: a,b,c,f,g,h,i Outcomes: a,b,c,d,e,f	Activities: a,b,c,e,f,h Outcomes: b,c,d,e,f,g,h,i,k	Outcomes: b,c,h,i
Wales	Range: 1,2,3,5 Skills: 1,2,3,4,5,6 Language Development: 3	Range: 1,2,3,4,6 Skills: 1,2 Language Development: 1	Range: 1,2,3,4,5,6,7 Skills: 1,2,3,4,5,6,7,8 Language Development: 1,2,3,4
NLS/NC	1d 2b 3e 4a	T2 T14 W2	T21
High Flier *The Story of Amy Johnson*			
Scotland	Level B/C	Level B/C	Level B/C
N. Ireland	Activities: a,b,c,f,g,h,i Outcomes: a,b,c,d,e,f	Activities: a,b,c,e,f,h Outcomes: b,c,d,e,f,g,h,i,k	Outcomes: b,c,h,i
Wales	Range: 1,2,3,5 Skills: 1,2,3,4,5,6 Language Development: 3	Range: 1,2,3,4,6 Skills: 1,2 Language Development: 1	Range: 1,2,3,4,5,6,7 Skills: 1,2,3,4,5,6,7,8 Language Development: 1,2,3,4
NLS/NC	1b 2d 3e 4a	T1 T17 W6	T19

Vocabulary chart

Alex Brychta *The Story of an Illustrator*	Years 1-2 High frequency words	about called came first good how just loved many more night once school some that them there these time very were when would
	Spelling strategies: compound words	everything everywhere notebooks playground compound words sketchbook suitcases understand
	Glossary words	animator Czech Czechoslovakia Prague invade publish Soviet Union
At the Top of the World *The Story of Tenzing Norgay*	Years 1-2 High frequency words	about again back could from help home last laughed many next night not over people than them then there too very want water when
	Spelling strategies: two syllables	climbers, crumbling, highest, hundred, mountain, thousand
	Glossary words	Chomolungma lama Miyosanglangma monastery Sherpa
Travels with Magellan *The Story of Ferdinand Magellan*	Years 1-2 High frequency words	about again another called could down from good helped here home jumped just last little live made many more new now one out people seen some take their them then three time took us very want water way when where with
	Spelling patterns: suffixes -ly, -ful	finally friendly sadly suddenly
	Glossary words	Pacific Ocean Patagonia route sawdust spice Spice Islands voyage
Ocean Adventure *The Story of Joshua Slocum*	Years 1-2 High frequency words	about again back been but called came first from home laughed loved make man more must new night many more new now one out people seen some take now old one out over people put ran saw than that their then three very wanted water way what when where with
	Spelling patterns: silent consonants	ache anchor dinghy island whirled wreck wrong
	Glossary words	anchor chart dinghy hurricane ocean
The Underground Railroad *The Story of Harriet Tubman*	Years 1-2 High frequency words	again back brother but by called came could from helped house jumped made many now old once one night ran saw take than that their there these too wanted way were with would when who
	Spelling strategies: three syllables	slavery plantation conductor dangerous
	Glossary words	plantation slave slave owner state
High Flier *The Story of Amy Johnson*	Years 1-2 High frequency words	about after again back been but by came could did down first from how last more next night not now our over people put so some take than that this time very wanted way were with would
	Spelling strategies: words with -ght	brought flight night sight straight thought
	Glossary words	ground engineer horizon pilot's licence propeller record route

Alex Brychta
The Story of an Illustrator

Group and independent reading activities

Introducing the story
Find the title and read it together. *Who is the author? What do you know about the author? What do you already know about*
- *Alex Brychta?*
- Look on the back cover and read the information there.
  Find the glossary. Read the words and their meanings. *Which*
- *words do you already know? Which are new words?*
  Read the introduction together.

During reading

Observing • reads text aloud with intonation and expression appropriate to the grammar and punctuation S1

Invite one child to read a few pages of the story aloud. Notice whether the child takes account of commas, question marks and other punctuation and reads with expression. Praise the child for reading fluently and independently. If there are any problems, remind the child to use phonics, syllables and the sense of the sentence to help.

Comprehension

Objective T13 understand the distinction between fact and fiction

- Read the introduction again. Ask the children to tell you three facts about Alex from this page.
- *Are the stories about Biff, Chip and Kipper fact or fiction? How do you know?*
- Find page 14. Which sentence tells us that Biff, Chip and Kipper are not real people?
- Find 11. *How do you think the author knows what Alex's teacher said to him?*
- Find three facts from the timeline on pages 22 and 23.

Assessment points	• Were the children able to select facts from the introduction and from the timeline? • Could they explain why Biff, Chip and Kipper are fiction? • Can the children explain how the author knew what to write about Alex?

Using spelling strategies

Objective	**W2** reinforce work on discriminating syllables from previous term (using compound words) e.g. *everything, everywhere*, etc.

- Use the list of compound words from the story (see table on page 4).
- Ask the children to separate each word in to two parts: *every thing; note books; play ground; suit cases; etc.*
- Look at each shorter word and try to think of another compound word that uses it, e.g. *everybody; nothing; playtime; underground; etc*
- Make a list of the new half words you have used.
- Try to make a compound word chain where you use half of one word in the next, e.g. *everything – nothing – nobody – somebody – sometime – playtime – playground – underground – understand.*

Assessment points	• Can the children split a compound word into two shorter words? Can they use the shorter words to generate more compound words? • Who understands the idea of a chain and can suggest suitable words?

Speaking and listening activities

Objectives	1b) choose words with precision; 2e) ask questions to clarify their understanding 3b) relate their contribution to what has gone before; 4b) create and sustain roles individually and when working with others
Cross-curricular links	Art and Design: *Knowledge and understanding: 4c differences and similarities in the work of artists, craftspeople and designers working in different times and cultures*

Responding to the book

Ask the children these questions to find out what they remember:
Why did Alex come to England?
What kind of work did his parents do?

What kind of artist did Alex train to be?
Why did he start to draw Biff, Chip and Kipper?

Personal experiences/Cross-curricular links

Look at some books that Alex has illustrated. *What do you like about them? What is special about them? How does Alex draw people's faces? If you looked at a pile of books, how would you recognize Alex's illustrations?*

Look at a variety of book illustrations. *In which ways are they like Alex's pictures? In which ways are they different?*

Role-play

Ask four children to pretend to be Alex's family.

- Arrange four chairs as if they were seats in a car. Decide where to sit by looking at the picture on pages 8 and 9. *Which side does the driver sit?*
- Ask each of the characters questions, beginning with:
  What is your name?
- Then ask different questions of each person, e.g.
  Why are you leaving your home?
  What have you brought with you?
  What did you have to leave behind?
  How do you feel at this minute?
- Ask the class or group if they have any questions to ask. The characters answer by using the information in the book and guessing what it was like to be in that situation.

Writing

Objective	**T19** to make simple notes from non-fiction texts, e.g. key words and phrases, page numbers

- Find out about the different work Alex did by reading from Chapter 5 onwards.
- Make a note of the job and the page number, e.g. Illustrated a book about Spain – page 12.
- Skim through the rest of the book and add the other work to your notes.
- Use your notes to tell the group what Alex did in England.
- You could use your notes to complete these sentences: "When Alex was 16…" "When he grew up ….." "Roderick Hunt asked Alex to …….." "Alex has worked with Roderick Hunt for ……."

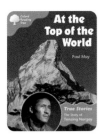

At the Top of the World
The Story of Tenzing Norgay

Group and independent reading activities

Introducing the story
Read the information on the cover and look at the picture.
Why do you think Tenzing Norgay is remembered?

- Read the introduction together.
  What do we call the highest mountain in the world?
- Find "Chomolungma" on page 5. Read the word in syllables.
- Find the glossary on page 24. Read all the words and their definitions.

During reading

Observing	• uses phonological, contextual, grammatical and graphic knowledge to work out, predict and check the meanings of unfamiliar words and to make sense of what they read T2

Ask children in turn to read a few pages to you. Notice how they tackle the long multi-syllabic words. Are they systematic about breaking the words into syllables? Do they leave out syllables? If necessary, show the child how to look at and read one syllable at a time. Praise children for reading these difficult words accurately.

Comprehension

Objective	**T13** use the terms "fact", "fiction" and "non-fiction" appropriately.

Ask these questions:
Would you find this book in the "fiction" or "non-fiction" part of a library or bookshop? How do you know where it belongs?
Can you think of a book that would be in the "fiction" section?
Does anyone know what the word "biography" means? Is it the same as a story?
Find facts about Tenzing's life from the story:
Where did he live? (page 4)
What was the date when Tenzing saved Edmund Hillary's life?
What was the date and time when they stood on the summit?

Assessment points	• Could the children explain how they separate books into "fiction" or "non-fiction"?
	• Could the children use the book to answer the questions about Tenzing's life?

Looking for spelling patterns

Objective	**W2** reinforce work on discriminating syllables from previous term (words with two syllables)

- Use the list of words with two syllables from the story (chart on page 4).
- Separate each word into syllables: *climb/ers, moun/tain, hun/dred*.
- Work in pairs to practise spelling the words syllable by syllable.
- First, listen to the syllables. Then ask one child to spell the first syllable and write it on the board. Ask the rest of the group if they agree. Use the opportunity to discuss the possible phonemes, e.g. is "ou" in "thou/sand" spelled "ou" or "ow"? Which pattern looks right?
- Then ask the second child to spell the second syllable to complete the word. Again, ask the rest of the group for their opinions.
- Finally, check the whole word by looking in the book.
- Practise spelling two syllable words from dictation. You could read out other words from the story, e.g. *climbers, highest, hundred*.

Assessment points	• Were the children able to break each word into two syllables?
	• Were they able to use their knowledge of phonemes?
	• Were there any misunderstandings?

Speaking and listening activities

Objectives	1d) focus on the main points; 2c) remember specific points that interest them; 3b) relate their contribution to what has gone on before; 4b) create and sustain roles individually and when working with others
Cross-curricular links	Geography: *Knowledge and understanding of places: 3b identify and describe where places are*

Responding to the story
What was special about Chomolungma?
Why did the climbers have to carry so much with them?
Who did Tenzing save from a fall?
Why did they have to sleep on the mountain?

Personal experiences/Cross-curricular links
- Use atlases to find maps of Nepal and the Himalayas. Ask the children to locate and name nearby countries. *What are the names of the nearest cities?* Find the name of the continent.
- Have any of the children visited Asia? Which countries?

Role-play
- Prepare questions for a news interview with Tenzing Norgay. Make a list on a board. For example:
  Why did you want to climb Chomolungma?
  How does it feel to stand on the highest mountain in the world?
  What was the worst part?
- Discuss each question and answer with the group. What might Tenzing say?
- Choose someone to be Tenzing and someone to interview him. You could use a "microphone".
- Ask the children to think of some more questions, bearing in mind what they have already heard.

Writing

Objective	**S6** turn statements into questions, learning a range of "wh" words typically used to open questions: what, where, when, who and to add question marks.

Write a quiz
- Begin on page 4. Ask the children to change the first sentence into a question, e.g. Who was Tenzing Norgay? Make the next two sentences into a "what?" question.
- Read the first sentence on page 6. Ask the children to change it into a "where?" question.
- Ask children to make the first sentence on page 11 into a "when" question.
- Write all the questions on the board.
- Ask the children to write three more questions.

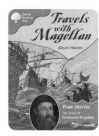

Travels with Magellan
The Story of Ferdinand Magellan
Group and independent reading activities

Introducing the story

Read the title and blurb. Look through the book for first impressions.

Talk about the writing. *Why do you think it is written like this? Is it about someone from the present or from the past?*

- Read the words and definitions listed in the glossary. *Which words are new? Which words do you already know?*
- Read the introduction together.
- Turn to page 4. *Why does the story begin with "I"?*

During reading

Observing • apply word level skills through shared and guided reading T1

Ask each child to read a chapter aloud. Notice how they cope with new words. Praise children for using initial sounds, known patterns and for breaking words into syllables. Remind children to reread the whole sentence if it does not seem to make sense.

Comprehension

Objective **T15** use a contents page and index to find way about a text

- Use the contents to find out how many countries the sailors visited.
- Choose one country each and turn to that chapter. Find one fact about what happened there. Read your fact to the group.
- Use the index to find out about food. Turn to one of the pages listed and find a fact to tell the group about the sailors' food.
- *Where were they when they had trouble with the storm?* Use the index to find out.
- *Where did the ships get covered in ice?* Use the index to find out.
- Find the dates of the voyage. How long were they away?

Assessment points
- Were the children able to use the contents and index to find the pages they needed?
- Could they identify relevant information on the pages?
- Did they skim the text to find what they needed, or did they read every page all through from the beginning?

Using spelling strategies

Objective W7 spell words with common suffixes, e.g.-ly

- Use the -ly words from the story listed on page 4. Write the words on the board.
- Ask a child to copy each word, leaving off the -ly; *sad, friend, sudden, final*. Read the new words together.
- Ask the children to close their eyes. Ask one child to spell one of the shorter words, e.g. "sad". Then ask another child to spell the word with -ly, e.g. "sadly". Practise spelling all four words in this way.
- Brainstorm a list of more -ly words that the children know, e.g. *slowly, crossly, quickly, safely, kindly, unfortunately*. Separate each word from its suffix and make a new list.
- You could use all your words without -ly to make a set of flash cards. Keep the cards for quick practice opportunities. Show the child a card, ask him or her to read it, then say the word with -ly. Hide the card while the child spells the word.

Assessment points
- Could the children copy each word, leaving off the -ly and read the new word?
- Could the children spell the shorter forms?
- Could the children generate more -ly words?

Speaking and listening activities

Objectives
1c) organize what they say;
2c) make relevant comments;
3e) give reasons for opinions;
4b) create and sustain roles individually and when working with others

Cross-curricular links
History:
breadth of study: 6c the lives of significant men, women and children drawn from the history of Britain and the wider world

Responding to the story
Where was Magellan trying to get to?
Can you guess why the Spice Islands were important?
Do you know the names of any spices?
Why did so many sailors die during the voyage?

Why did the voyage take so long?
What do you think about the way the book is printed? Do you think it makes the book more realistic? In what way?

Personal experiences/Cross-curricular links
Discuss what Magellan did that made him a great explorer. *What were the difficulties and hardships of sailing at that time? Imagine you were on that boat, what would be the best things about it? What would be the worst things? Can you understand why young men wanted to go to sea?*
Have you been on the sea in a ship or a sailing boat?
Would you want to go to sea in a modern boat? What would be good and bad about it? Do you know the names of anyone else who has sailed around the world?

Role-play
Read chapter 2 again together.
Talk about what the men might have said to Magellan to persuade him to go home. *Why did they not want to go on land? Did they have the right clothes for very cold weather? Why would they want to go home?*
Choose five or six children to be the crew and one child to be Magellan. Make the scene when they wanted to go home. Use the pictures on pages 8 and 9 to help. Ask each sailor to use one of the ideas to persuade Magellan to go home. Help Magellan decide what he says in reply.

Writing

Objective	**T20** to write non-fiction texts, using texts as models for own writing

Read pages 6 and 7 again. Think of some more wonderful animals, birds and fishes that a sailor might see for the first time. Make a list: dolphin, albatross, giraffe, crocodile, ostrich. Use the list to write descriptions: enormous seagulls that glided beside us; friendly blue fishes that followed our boat; tall birds that could run but not fly; animals with long necks that ate the tops of the trees; creatures with great jaws and sharp teeth that lurked in the rivers.
Ask the children to copy page 6 but change what they saw, using the ideas discussed. Copy page 7 but change what you gave the people and what the people gave you.
You could make old, brown paper by painting paper with cold tea. Display the pages from a sailor's diary.

Ocean Adventure
The story of Joshua Slocum

Group and independent reading activities

Introducing the story
Read the title and the "blurb".

Read the words in the glossary. *Which words do you already know?*

- Read the introduction together. *Why would someone want to sail around the world alone? What might the problems be?*
- Look through the pictures. *Were you right about some of the problems? Are there other problems or dangers?*

During reading

Observing • read text aloud with intonation and expression appropriate to the grammar and punctuation S1

Ask the children to read a chapter each. Notice whether the reader is aware when someone is speaking. Does the reader change expression to match what is being said? Does he or she notice when there is a question? Does he or she notice and respond to commas in a sentence? Praise the child for reading in an interesting way. If there are any difficulties remind the child to break the word into syllables and use phonics.

Comprehension

Objective **T7** compare books by different authors on similar themes; to evaluate, giving reasons

Questions about the story
What was special about Joshua's journey?
What do you remember about it?
How long ago was it?
What did you find out about Joshua's boat?

Questions about Joshua
What did he do when he was lonely? (page 7)
What mistakes did he make? (pages 13 and 20)
How did he protect the boat from pirates? (page16)
What did he do that was clever? (page 17)

Make comparisons
Think about another book about someone who travelled around the world (e.g. Travels with Magellan). *Which one did you like best?*

15

> Did you find out as much about the main character as you found out about Joshua?
> Did you like the main character as much, or more?
> Which book illustrates the journey most clearly?

Assessment points
- Could the children explain why they liked one book more than another?
- Could they compare the way the books showed the person's character?
- Could they make judgments about the illustrations?

Using spelling strategies

Objective
W8 new words from reading linked to particular topics (words with silent consonants)

- Use the list of words with silent consonants from page 4.
- Sort out the words that use the same letters, e.g. silent "w": *wreck, wrong*; silent "h": *ache, anchor, dinghy*: silent "s": *island*.
- Use a dictionary to add more words that begin with "wr". Make a list.
- Ask each child to choose five useful "wr" words and copy them, e.g. *wrap, wreck, write, writing, wrote*.
- Practise spelling the five words by using the "look, say, cover, write, check" method: Look at the first word, say the letters to yourself, turn over the paper and write it on the back. Then check.
- Test each other by reading a word from a partner's list. The partner says the spelling of the word while you check it.
Add to your lists of silent consonants as you find them.

Assessment points
- Notice how well children concentrate while learning their spellings.
- Can the children see whether a word looks right or not?

Speaking and listening activities

Objectives
1e) include relevant detail;
2b) remember specific points that interest them;
3e) give reasons for opinions;
4a) use language to explore and convey situations

Cross-curricular links
History:
breadth of study: 6c the lives of significant men, women and children drawn from the history of Britain and the wider world.

Responding to the story
What do you think was the most annoying part of the journey for Joshua?
What was the most dangerous? What were the happiest times? Can you find out how far he sailed and how long it took?
(page 23)

Personal experiences/Cross-curricular links
Talk about reasons for remembering Joshua Slocum. Think of all the difficulties involved in sailing a boat on your own. *What was more difficult about sailing a boat on your own a hundred years ago than today? Why is it difficult and dangerous to sail alone today? What would you be worried about? What would be wonderful about sailing alone?*

Role-play
Read page 16 again. Choose children to be Captain Slocum and the pirates. The Captain mimes spreading nails on the deck and going to sleep. The pirates mime rowing to the ship, climbing aboard, treading on the nails and getting away again.
Talk to one of the children quietly about different parts of the story: singing, being ill, trying to swim, reading while the ship steered itself. Ask that child to mime one of them for the others to guess. The person who guesses can be the captain next.

Writing

Objective	**W10** use synonyms and other alternative words/phrases that express same or similar meanings

Rewrite the last chapter
- Read the last chapter again together. Rewrite the sentence "Lightning crackled and thunder roared."
- Rewrite each sentence on page 22 together in this way.
Ask the children to change each sentence on page 23.

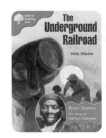

The Underground Railroad
The Story of Harriet Tubman

Group and independent reading activities

Introducing the story
Read the blurb on the cover and look through the pictures. Ask the children to think of questions that they think will be answered in the story, e.g. *What was the Underground Railroad? What was it like to be a slave?*
- Make a list of the children's questions.
- Ask the children to help you to spell the words as you write. Read the words in the glossary and their meanings.

During reading

Observing • uses phonological, contextual, grammatical and graphic knowledge to work out, predict and check the meanings of unfamiliar words and to make sense of what they read T2

Ask one child to read a few pages. If there are problem words, help the child by suggesting what to do, e.g. for "Pennsylvania" suggest that the child looks at each syllable, for "pretend" suggest using the letter sounds. Praise children for working out words by themselves, and for using a variety of clues.

Comprehension

Objective T14 to pose questions and record these in writing, prior to reading non-fiction to find answers.

- Use the questions written during the introduction.
- Go through the questions one at a time and answer them. Encourage the children to find the place in the book that has the answer. Reread that part to check your answer.
- Some questions will have the answers on more than one page, e.g. *What was it like to be a slave?* can be answered on pages 7, 8, 9, 10 and 11.
- Make a display of the questions. Ask the children to choose two questions that interest them and write the answers. Display the answers next to the questions.
- If a question cannot be answered, is there another book, or an internet site, that could give that information? Encourage the children to use other resources to find answers.

Assessment points	• Did the children think of appropriate questions? • Were they able to answer them after reading the book? • Were they able to find the page that gave the answer?

Using spelling strategies

Objective	**W2** reinforce work on discriminating syllables from previous term (words with three syllables)

- Use the list of words with three syllables from the chart on page 4.
- Ask the children to copy each word and put / lines to show the syllables, e.g. *sla/ver/y*
- Practice spelling each word using the look, say, cover, write, check method.
- Notice the "-tion" spelling pattern in "plantation". Think of some more "-tion" words, such as "station", "action", "fiction". Ask the children to have a go at spelling these words.
- Notice the "-ous" ending of "dangerous". Think of some more words with this ending, such as "nervous", "horrendous", "serious", "continuous".

Assessment points	• Could the children separate longer words into syllables? • Were they using the syllables to help work out and remember the spellings? • Who could suggest another word with the same spelling pattern?

Speaking and listening activities

Objectives	1d) focus on the main points; 2b) remember specific points that interest them; 3e) give reasons for opinions; 4a) use language to convey situations, characters and emotions
Cross-curricular links	History: *Breadth of study: 6c the lives of significant men, women and children drawn from the history of Britain and the wider world.*

Responding to the story

Why did Harriet have to work so hard?
Did Miss Susan work as hard?
What was unfair about owning slaves?
Why was Harriet brave to help on the Underground Railroad?
Why do you think it was called "underground"?

Personal experiences/Cross-curricular links

- Talk about reasons for remembering Harriet Tubman. *What was special about her life?* Think of a list of words that describe people we remember long after they have died, e.g. *brave, clever, unselfish, powerful*, etc. *Which of these words applied to Harriet?*
- *Suppose you had been Harriet, what would you have done?*

Role-play

- Think of questions to ask Miss Susan, such as:
  Why do you have slaves working for you?
  What do you think of Harriet?
- Ask someone to pretend to be Miss Susan. Take turns to ask the questions you have thought of.
- Think of questions to ask Harriet, such as:
  Why did you run away?
  How did you feel when you saw your old master in the street?
- Ask a volunteer to be Harriet. Take turns to ask Harriet these and other questions.

Writing

Objective **T21** write a non-chronological report

The Underground Railroad

- Read page 13 again. Find three facts that explain the railroad.
- Ask the children to tell you each fact in their own words.
- Scribe the beginning of the report. Reread it to show the children how to check that it says what you want it to.
- Find pages 16 and 17. Decide how to finish the sentence "When slaves reached a station, they ...." Add this sentence to the report.
- Find page 21. Find out what a conductor did. Write "conductors were important on the Underground Railroad because ......"
- Finish the report by explaining when the Underground Railroad was no longer needed. (page 23)

High Flier
The story of Amy Johnson

Group and independent reading activities

Introducing the story
Skim-read to speculate what the book might be about. Make a group list of predictions.

During reading

Observing • apply their word level skills through shared and guided reading T1

Comprehension

Objective **T17** to skim read title, contents page, illustrations, chapter headings to speculate what a book might be about

Refer back to introduction and group list of predictions. What was easy to predict? What did no-one predict? How much can you tell about a book without reading it?

Assessment points • How much were the children able to predict correctly about the story?

Using spelling strategies

Objective **W6** words which have the same spelling patterns but different sounds.

- Use the -ght words from the story: *brought, flight, night, sight, straight, thought.*
  Sort them out into lists of words that rhyme.
- Think of some more words to add to the "flight" rhyming list, e.g. *bright, tight, light.*
- Think of some more words with -ough that do not rhyme, such as *through, tough, dough, cough, rough.*
- Choose five words from the lists to learn the spellings. Use the "look, say, cover, write" method to learn the words.
- Work with a partner to test each other's spelling.

Assessment points	• Were the children aware of rhyming words in the list? • Could they think of some more words to rhyme with "flight"? • Did they learn their spellings successfully?

Speaking and listening activities

Objectives	1b) choose words with precision; 2d) listen to others' reactions; 3e) give reasons for opinions and actions; 4a) use language to explore and convey situations
Cross-curricular links	History: Breadth of study: 6c the lives of significant men, women and children drawn from the history of Britain and the wider world

Responding to the story
Do you remember the name of Amy's aeroplane?
Why did Amy need to be an engineer as well as a pilot?
Why did she have to keep stopping?
Why didn't she break the record?
How long did it take Amy to fly to Australia?

Personal experiences/Cross-curricular links
Ask the children to think of a time when they have done something for the first time, e.g. swimming a length, riding a bike, acting in a play.
How did you feel just before you tried something new?
How did you feel afterwards?
Think of reasons why Amy Johnson should be remembered. *What did she achieve? Why was she special?*

Role-play
Meeting the press
Imagine what it was like for Amy to talk to reporters when she landed in Australia. Think of the questions that they would ask. You could make a list to remind the children of the kinds of things to ask. Think about how Amy would have been feeling: *tired, dirty, hungry, excited, happy, proud.* Ask a volunteer to be Amy. Take turns to ask Amy questions. After four or five questions, ask for a different volunteer to be Amy.

Writing

Objective — **T19** make simple notes from non-fiction texts, e.g. headings to use in subsequent writing

Amy's adventure
- Talk about the difficulties and dangers Amy met on her journey around the world. *What do you remember?*
- Find the first difficulty on page 12. Think of a heading that would sum this up, e.g. "Low Cloud East of Turkey", or 'Lost in the clouds'.
- On page 15 think of a similar heading for the next problem.
- On page 18 decide upon a heading to sum up the petrol problem
- On page 21 Amy crashes into goal posts. Think of a heading for this incident.
- Finally, on page 22, think of a heading for the last long flight.
- Use these headings as chapters. Write the story independently, or use the headings to retell the major hazards of the flight orally.

Links to other Oxford Reading Tree titles

Branch Library Non-fiction Stages 8-10 *Reds* packs A and B
Branch Library Biographies: *What's Their Story?*
Pack A Stages 10-13; pack B Stages 10-14
Fact Finders units D, E and F

OXFORD
UNIVERSITY PRESS

Great Clarendon Street, Oxford OX2 6DP

Oxford University Press is a department of the University of Oxford. It furthers the University's objective of excellence in research, scholarship, and education by publishing worldwide in

Oxford   New York

Auckland Cape Town Dar es Salaam Hong Kong Karachi
Kuala Lumpur Madrid Melbourne Mexico City Nairobi
New Delhi Shanghai Taipei Toronto

With offices in
Argentina Austria Brazil Chile Czech Republic France Greece
Guatemala Hungary Italy Japan Poland Portugal Singapore
South Korea Switzerland Thailand Turkey Ukraine Vietnam

Oxford is a registered trade mark of Oxford University Press in the UK and in certain other countries© Oxford University Press 2003

The moral rights of the author have been asserted

Database right Oxford University Press (maker)

First published 2003

All rights reserved. No part of this publication may be reproduced, stored in a retrieval system, or transmitted, in any form or by any means, without the prior permission in writing of Oxford University Press, or as expressly permitted by law, or under terms agreed with the appropriate reprographics rights organization. Enquiries concerning reproduction outside the scope of the above should be sent to the Rights Department, Oxford University Press, at the address above

You must not circulate this book in any other binding or cover and you must impose this same condition on any acquirer

British Library Cataloguing in Publication Data

Data available

Cover illustrations Alex Brychta

Teacher's Notes: ISBN: 978-0-19-919697-5

10 9 8

Page make-up by IFA Design Ltd, Plymouth, Devon

Printed in China by Imago